GOD

THE

IRRESISTIBLE

I.D. Campbell

ISBN: 978-1478360995

ISBN: 1478360992

DEDICATION

John L. Campbell, Arlene W. Campbell, Calvin Campbell, Jasmine Campbell, Latrina Campbell, Ishmael Campbell II, Nasir Campbell

This is also dedicated to all the men and women of the past, present and future who have and who will shed blood, sweat and tears to convey the message of the one true God. It is a hard road, but it is one worth travelling.

CONTENTS

ACKNOWLEDGMENTS

First and foremost, Alhamdulillah. All praise is due to Allah. He is the source of all truth, therefore all that I convey of the truth in this book and in life are because of Allah, and only the mistakes are from me.

Introduction

When I was in the 9th grade, I had a history teacher who was a professing atheist. He was obviously outspoken because his beliefs about God were given voluntarily since American history had nothing to do with his ideas about God. He felt that it was necessary to express his lack of belief in God. Around the 9th grade was the time that I began an awakening in my thinking about God and about the world. My history teacher had sparked my interest and I remember challenging his belief in class and after class. I vividly recall a friendly debate between he and I about God's existence in the school library. My argument hinged on two points, the need for God to exist and the desire for God to exist.

The need for God comes from the existence of everything. My teacher subscribed to the Big Bang theory, so I asked him to explain the theory to me. He said that there were some gases that combined and caused a big bang. I stopped him there and asked, where did the gases come from? He had no answer. I asked him, what made the gases combine? He had no answer. I said that you need God to explain your belief in the origin of this universe. He said nothing. As he thought, I recalled that we had recently discussed Adolf Hitler in class. I said Hitler killed himself before he was captured and brought to justice for killing 6 million Jews. I said to my teacher with your belief system, he will never be held accountable. In my belief system, he will be punished for his heinous crimes. In fact, all good people will be rewarded for the good that they have done and all bad people will be punished for what they have done. I asked him to put aside which system, atheism or theism, he believes to be true, and answer which system he preferred to be true. He was forced to admit that, in this instance, he preferred that theism be true. Though he did not concede any further I was content with the discussion that we had. At about 14 years old, I did not know then how much more evidence there is for God, nor did I know how prevalent atheism would become.

Maybe five years ago, in my efforts to propagate Islam, I inadvertently pushed a theist into atheism. The man was one amongst many Christians that I was debating with online. He was going to college to become a minister, and ministers are privy to information that everyday Christians are unaware of. When the other Christians and I were disputing points about the Christian Trinity, he would be forced to admit that I was speaking the truth. Apparently this weighed heavily on his conscience, so much so that he renounced Christianity and he declared himself an atheist. The website that we were on crashed and when it returned I found out about his conversion. I made a thread dedicated to him and I sent him private messages in an effort to assure him that because one belief system is inaccurate, this is not grounds to discount all systems of belief, especially the belief in God. His presence on the site had always been sporadic, but it became clear that he had abandoned the site. I must admit that his conversion had a profound effect on me. I realized that one should not disprove a person's belief without giving the person a clear alternative. I should have reiterated the true monotheism of Islam as an alternative to the paradoxical monotheism of the Trinity. After this experience, I have made a conscious effort to point out that God's existence should not be in dispute at all. This book is the culmination of the most compelling scientific evidence for God.

Simple Deduction

In today's time, it has become fashionable to deny the existence of God. Of course, I am a theist. I believe that God is the creator and sustainer of the universe. But there are agnostics. They say that it is impossible to know if God exists or not. Agnosticism's latin root means "not known." Then there are atheists. They deny the existence of God. The latin root for atheism means "no god." Though both groups insist they do not have a belief system, this is completely untrue. From their declaration as an agnostic or an atheist, we can easily derive their belief system. For example, an agnostic or someone who believes that it is impossible to know whether a creator exists or not, he must believe:

1. that it is possible for something to come into being without a cause.

2. that it is possible that something can come from complete nothingness.
3. that it is possible for organized information to come about by random events (chance).
4. that it is possible for life to come from the non-living.
5. that it is possible for life to come about by random events (chance).

An atheist or someone who believes that there is no creator, he must believe

1. that something did come into being without a cause.
2. that the universe did come into existence from nothing and by nothing.
3. that organized information did come about by random events (chance).
4. that life did come from the non-living.
5. that life did come about by random events (chance).

I submit to you that no one believes the premises of atheists and I will show that the probability for the agnostic's premises is so astronomical that no reasonable person would believe in these mere possibilities. There is no agnostic or atheist who would admit to believing these things, yet the title that they place on themselves requires these premises to be true. Any fluctuation on any of these five points means that they can no longer call themselves agnostics or atheists in all honesty. Any person who leaves the slightest possibility for a

Creator is not an atheist. He is an agnostic. And any agnostic who does not believe in the possibility of any one of my five premises is no longer an agnostic. He is at the very least a deist. I will show that the bare minimum of belief for any thinking person is in deism and that even deism is not a sufficient explanation for the world around us and the world within us. I will show that agnosticism is the discontinuing of the thought process on the subject of this universe's origin and the origin of life and that atheism is nothing more than wishful thinking. The probing of one who subscribes to these titles will ultimately lead to the revelation that they are not agnostics or atheists at all. I will also demonstrate the rational, reasonable, scientific, sensible and logical conclusion of those who believe in the Creator of the universe.

The End of Atheism

"Since 1979, you will not find in peer review journals the fact that life started by random reaction. You will always find that a catalyst is REQUIRED, FORCE IS REQUIRED. Something is required in the environment that forces the life to occur." - Dr. Gerald Schoeder, the physicist who was instrumental in converting the Famous Atheist Anthony Flew to deism

A theist once said "most people can't even organize a checkbook and you consider them both conscious and intelligent. But here we have a force that is organizing the entire cosmos, including trillions and trillions of species on the planet earth alone, and their environments, but somehow this force is neither conscious nor intelligent. Does that really make sense to you?"

Our universe is expanding. This is a scientific fact. Now what can we deduce from this fact? We can deduce that, if we peer back into time, our universe would get smaller and smaller the further we look back. Thus the universe was at one point a "singularity" as famous physicist Stephen Hawking has named it. The phenomenon which caused this singularity to expand is called the Big Bang. Two scientists, Dr. Arno A. Perzias and Dr. Robert W. Wilson, won the Nobel Prize for their discovery of cosmic microwave background radiation (CMBR). CMBR is the remnants of radiation remaining as a result of the Big Bang. The static that you hear on your radio when you change the channels is your radio picking up that background radiation's sound waves. Therefore the Big Bang theory is only theory in exactly how the Big Bang happened. That a big explosion took place is not in question amongst scientists.

Explosions are generally used for destruction, yet this explosion CONSTRUCTED the universe. The constructive explosions that we know of today are planned and executed by intelligent living beings, humans. How much more intelligent is the being that constructed the universe from an explosion? But all explosions, whether destructive or constructive, have a cause. And there are two types of causes, mechanical and personal.

A mechanical cause is like a pool stick hitting the cue ball, which hits that 8 ball and goes into the pocket. A personal cause has free will, so it would be the man who used the pool stick to hit the cue ball. Now all mechanical causes REQUIRE a personal cause, because pool balls won't hit each other without a free willed personal cause which is outside of the mechanical system. The Big Bang is a mechanical cause which began a mechanical system. Photons began to cause friction and heat, and protons and electrons combined to form hydrogen atoms. This is the beginning of the Big Bang, but photons, protons and electrons do not have free will. They don't move by themselves, thus a personal cause is REQUIRED for the process to begin.

I have been in discussion with many people who find this difficult to understand due to their belief in atheism. They attempt to find effects which do not have a personal cause. They postulate that the wind blows without cause, lightning flashes without cause and stars explode without cause. The problem is that all these elements of nature exist in a mechanical system. Though stars are billions of years old and their explosion may come after billions of years, this does not negate that its explosion was caused. As an explosion is an effect, it must have a cause. Its cause was the Big Bang and the formation of the universe, which warranted it a set lifespan. At the end of that lifespan it explodes or implodes. You see, there is a rule which pertains to something coming into existence. That is, everything that comes into existence has a cause. Things do not pop up out of thin air. Have you ever sat in your living room and a pony just appeared from nowhere? No and this will never happen.

Did lightning or wind always exist? The answer is no. Thus it requires a cause. Does lightning decide where it will strike? Does the wind decide which way it will blow? They both are subject to the laws of nature. They do not have free will. The same is true of any chemical reaction or the combining of any chemicals. They don't decide to combine themselves arbitrarily. All these elements follow a process, a system and systems necessitate a personal cause. For example, I hit a golf ball that goes through a tube. Then the golf ball hits a button that starts a fan, which turns on a radio. What some are doing is staying fixated on the fan and the radio. My point is that none of the system will work without a personal cause hitting that golf ball at the beginning. And you can add what you like in my system, like a chair falls that hits the golf ball. The system still requires a personal cause to have the chair move. Or let's say the golf ball goes in the tube and it makes a sound that wakes the neighbor's dog. The sound waves may be unintentional, but they are not free willed. They still require a cause. I mention this because some atheists, realizing their dilemma, have suggested that creation may have be an accident done by the Creator. Their acknowledgement makes them a deist, and we will soon see whether this universe and its existence were planned or not. But we can go a bit further with the formation of the universe.

We can go ahead of the Big Bang. Scientists tell us that the universe is 13.8 billion years old. That means that 13.8 billion years and one second ago, the universe DID NOT EXIST. It came into existence and everything that comes into existence has a CAUSE. Some atheists have used an idea called infinite regress as an alternative to the Big Bang origin of the universe. This idea suggests that the universe has always existed, but this is no more than faith. It is a belief without proof or evidence. It is what some people wish and hope is true. Belief in infinite regress is a religion and a completely unscientific one at that, due to the fact that the universe is almost 13.8 billion years old. And scientists know the approximate age of the universe by studying the cosmic microwave background radiation (CMBR) in the universe's atmosphere. So before the Big Bang, nothing that we see, hear, smell, taste, or feel existed. Nothing in the universe existed. This universe, and everything in it, was non-existent.

"And so, from nothing, our universe begins"-Bill Bryson, _A Short History of Nearly Everything_

There was complete nothingness. No time and no space. And from nothing, the components of the universe came into being. Think about something coming from nothing. What is the difference between one and zero? In math, it is but one because both numbers are abstract. Zero is not actually real, it is actually nothing. So the real question is, what is the difference between one of something existent and of something non-existent? And the difference is infinite. It is immeasurable. Today we witness things that were not thought of or dreamed of years ago. For example, a plasma television was not conceived of 200 years ago. Though the people of that time didn't have the knowledge or the technology, they did have the resources to make a plasma television. But 13.8 billion years ago, there were no resources. There were no stars, no moon, and no planets to put in orbit. There was nothing and then there was something. How awesome must the power be to create a universe from nothing at all?

Sir Isaac Newton, the brilliant scientist and noted theist, discovered the law of cause and effect, which shows that every effect has a cause. Because of this law, we can see that a personal cause outside of the universe, a mechanical system, caused the universe to come into existence. And this personal cause is not subject to the laws of the universe because it is outside of the universe and it created the laws to start with. The law of gravity, the laws of nature, and the law of cause and effect are laws of this universe. The creator created these laws. Before he created them, they did not exist. Therefore he is not subject to them. He is not subject to nature, thus he is supernatural. He does not grow or diminish. He does not need food or drink, shelter or sleep. And he is not subject to cause and effect. So the question who caused or who created God is a nonsensical one. The creator created creation. The causer caused cause to exist. Scientists call him the First Cause.

They deduce that there must be an infinite being which created the finite universe. And his existence is NECESSARY for our existence and the existence of the universe.

This is an irrefutable fact. Those who call themselves atheists write books and give lectures arguing against a religious or a personal God, not against God in general as a supernatural being which brought the universe into existence. This is because they can't. Astrophysicist Neil deGrasse Tyson has stated in a lecture that about 40% of all scientists believe in a personal God and 85% of the elite scientists (members of the National Academy of Sciences) reject the idea of a personal God. 15% of the elite scientists believe in a personal God. But he did not mention the percentage of scientists, elite or otherwise, who believe in a creator. This is very telling. This information is vital to the laymen's understanding when they consider that atheism is a viable option to theism. They place their faith in scientists' opinion, when some scientists are not honestly presenting their position. Very few, if anyone, scientist or otherwise, will commit to disbelief in a Creator of our universe, they will clout their deism by denying the existence of a personal God.

Atheists often accuse those who believe in God of ignoring science in order to continue with their beliefs. Of course, we are now finding that science is the basis for our belief in God and that many atheists had been opposed to the implications of recent scientific findings. Scientists like English astronomer Arthur Eddington, the German chemist Walter Nernst, and MIT professor of physics Phillip Morrison, all publicly admitted their desire for the Big Bang theory to be false (see Harun Yahya's "Timelessness and the Reality of Fate"). Why would an unbiased scientist WANT a theory to be false? It is because they are not unbiased. They are atheists with a dogma that they want to be true. They realize the implications of a huge explosion which began from nothing. They realize that the elements of the Big Bang had to come from somewhere and that a Big Bang must be started by someone.

The atheist evangelist Richard Dawkins, in his book "The God Delusion" describes himself as 6/7ths of an atheist. What does that mean? I am not 3/4ths of a theist. The reason that he has levels of atheism is because he is not really an atheist. He has admitted in his own book that he is not fully convinced that God doesn't exist, which means that he is not an atheist. He is a wishful agnostic or a deist. He wishes that God doesn't exist, thus his book's title is disingenuous. It should be "Maybe God is a Delusion" or "God is a Delusion, Hopefully." I have seen him fair quite poorly in debate on whether God is a delusion (against Professor John Lennox), yet he obliviously continues his mission. In fact, he is recorded as saying that there can be a valid case for Intelligent Design. He even speculates that an alien life form could have planted life on earth. He obviously understands the great dilemma that atheists have with the emergence of life and its need for an agent to produce this life. Unfortunately, he only makes his problem more complicated when he injects the existence of another life form because their life must also have a source. Only a living being outside of this universe and its law could have produced life within this universe. The same is true for theory of multiple universes or multiverses. There cannot be an infinite amount of universes in which we are a part. Time is not infinite. If you meet a person who entertains the idea of an infinite universe or infinite universes, ask them to count to three for you, using negative infinity. They will not be able to get to the number three. They will not be able to start counting at all. So if the universe's beginning was infinite, then we would never get to this moment in time right now. And universes are not personal causes, they are mechanical so however many universes some hope scientists will find one day, they will ALWAYS REQUIRE a personal cause.

The End of Agnosticism

"Can we really get a biological cell by waiting for time and chance and combinations of organic compounds? This would require more time than the universe might EVER see, if chance and random combination were the only driving force for life." Wald also said "that it has occurred to him that quantum physics has shown that the origin of consciousness and the origin of life come from mind and that mind is responsible for the creation of the universe." -George Wald's (an American scientist who won a share of the 1967 Nobel Prize in Physiology or Medicine.)

At this point, it is safe to say that an atheist confronted with this evidence has sole refuge in the stance of agnosticism. This is where you meet people who call themselves "agnostic atheist" which means that they believe it is impossible to know if God exists, but they hope that he doesn't. So now is the time to expound on probabilities because the agnostic believes in the mere possibility that the universe is uncaused, that something can come from nothing, etc. But are these possibilities and probabilities reasonable to believe. It is also possible that some man in Uzbekistan is your father. But who believes that? Yes a paternity test can say with 100% accuracy that someone is not your father, but it is 99.99% accurate when it identifies your actual father. This means that there is a slight possibility that the man that you call your father is not actually your father. That chance is .01%. (1 in 10,000 men in the population). There are 6.8 billion people on earth and over 300 million people in the U.S. alone, yet 99.99% accuracy is legally sufficient in a court of law. Though it is possible, it is highly improbable that anyone else is the paternal father. Now how does this pertain to God? Let us first explore our DNA.

"Human DNA contains more organized information than the Encyclopedia Britannica."
-George Sim Johnson

When you meet an agnostic ask them, "If you found an encyclopedia, would you believe that it came into existence by time and chance?" It is critical to have them answer this question because they will attempt to latch on to the fact that it is possible. It is possible, but it is so incredibly improbable that they do not believe that it is true. The agnostic will be forced to admit that he does not believe that an encyclopedia can come about by time and chance. An encyclopedia is

-a reference work (often in several volumes) containing articles on various topics (often arranged in alphabetical order) ***dealing with the entire range of human knowledge*** or with some particular specialty

DNA is a microscopic encyclopedia, which means that the agnostic must also denounce the mere possibility that it came into existence randomly. In this case, it is important to differentiate between organized information and complexity. You are not just saying that DNA is complex, but that it contains a collection of facts or data (information) functioning within a formal structure (organized). Collecting of facts denotes intelligence. So too does constructing a formal structure. Thus the combination of these two things increases the unlikelihood that they came about randomly.

Some scientists suggest that the idea of Intelligent Design does not lend itself to testing, so they don't even considering its validity. They deem any explanation that is without a means to prove that it is false to be unworthy of their attention. However this is the furthest from the truth. Ask an agnostic to provide ONE example of sequenced data or organized information that is not a product of intelligence. This would prove that Intelligent

Design is not necessary for the development of organized information. He cannot provide one example because its possibility is so extremely unlikely that there is no example in nature for it. It is beyond the realm of reason to believe that the microscopic DNA came about by chance. Ironically these same scientists who assert that Intelligent Design is not falsifiable are busy trying to prove that it is false, while they are proponents of a theory which fits the bill for not being falsifiable. They state that some unintelligent process produced organized information. This would require that one prove all possible processes are false, which is actually impossible. So it is their ideology which should be unworthy of their attention, let alone their acceptance. Intelligence is the only explanation for the existence of organized information in DNA. What about the building block of life, protein?

Protein is absolutely essential for life. Every living thing is composed of protein from the largest animal to a single-celled organism. After water, protein makes up the greatest part of the human body. Protein is responsible for everything from growth of muscles and bones to the repairing of tissue and cells. The genetic code in the cell's DNA is actually information on how to make the cell's protein. Thus the protein is required to make cells, and it has, within the cell, a mechanism to be regenerated. A protein is a compound composed of carbon, hydrogen, oxygen and nitrogen. These four elements are arranged as strands of amino acids, which are the building blocks of protein. These strands of amino acids linked together in a chain. The chain may contain as many as 2 amino acid units or as many as 3,000. There are only 20 different types of amino acids in the human body, and they only become proteins when 50 or more amino acids are joined in a chain. Think of the 26 letters in the alphabet. They combine to make a multitude of words. And just as the same letters can be used multiple times in a word and in a sentence, so too can those 20 amino acids be used multiple times to form a very lengthy chain.

Each type of protein is composed of a specific group of amino acids in a specific chemical arrangement and proteins are not interchangeable. They are tailored for the body's specific needs. Of those 20 amino acids needed for the human body to build protein, only 12 are made within the body. The other 8 are obtained through diet. When we eat food, the body actually breaks down the protein from our food into amino acids. And the body uses those amino acids to build the specific proteins that it needs. All of this is expressed to demonstrate the intricate system by which life came to be. The building block of life, protein, is based upon another building block, amino acids, which are based upon a specific combination of 50 or more strands of carbon, hydrogen, oxygen and nitrogen. And to further illustrate the magnitude of life's existence, we must try to wrap our minds around the fact that there are approximately 2 million different types of protein in the human body. So the combinations of amino acids must be precise for every single type of protein. Now what is the probability that one protein out of 2 million was formed by chance?

We must first realize that for every probability there is a counter probability. So if it is a 1 in 100 chance that you will drop this book out of your hands, there is a 99 in 100 chance that you will not. The reasonable person will chose the 99% chance.

"When trying to determine whether the desired results will happen, always consider that the fractions used in probabilities carry two stories with them. One tells you the chance of something happening, and the other tells you the chance that that same event will not happen; i.e., if the odds are one in ten (10%) that a certain event will occur, then likewise the odds are nine to ten (90%) that it will not...

Who could reasonably believe that a coin will turn up heads 100 times in succession, when the odds for it happening are: 1 in 1,000,000,000,000,000,000,000,000,000,000...and the probability that it won't is: 999,999,999,999,999,999,999,999,999,999 in 1,000,000,000,000,000,000,000,000,000,000...The probability that the event will not happen is what we must believe if we are concerned about being realistic."

-(R. L. Wysong, The Creation-Evolution Controversy, pp. 80-81. As quoted on Apologetics Press.org by Dr. Bert Thompson and Dr. Brad Harrub.)

We have said that it takes at least 50 amino acids to make a protein. But the largest known protein in the human body, the titin, is a combination of 26,926 amino acids. To be moderate, let us say that a given protein has 100 combinations of the 20 amino acids. The probability that ONE PROTEIN arose randomly and by chance is 1 in 20^{100} or 10^{130}.

"First, you need the right bonds between amino acids. Second, amino acids come in right-handed and left-handed versions, and you've got to get only left-handed ones. Third, the amino acids must link up in a specific sequence, like letters in a sentence. Run the odds of these things falling into place on their own and find that the probabilities of forming a rather short functional protein at random would be one chance in a hundred thousand trillion trillion trillion trillion trillion trillion trillion trillion trillion trillion. That's a ten with 125 zeroes (10^{125}) after it! And that would only be one protein molecule-a minimally complex cell would need between three hundred and five hundred protein molecules. Plus, all of this would have to be accomplished in mere 100 million years, which is the approximate window of time between the Earth cooling and the first microfossils we've found. To suggest chance against those odds is really to invoke a naturalistic miracle."(Stephen C. Meyer, PHD in Lee Strobel's, "The Case for a Creator")

The famed astronomer, astrophysicist, cosmologist and author Carl Sagan estimated this probability to be approximately 1 in 10^{130} (Carl Sagan, Encyclopaedia Britannica). Well according to Borel's Law of mathematically probability, anything with a probability less than 1 in 10^{50} is **"mathematically impossible**." This is because scientists believe there have been much less that 10^{50} chemical combinations since the emergence of life on earth. Therefore it would be impossible for an event to occur which required more than 10^{50} combinations. So the idea that one protein came about randomly with its probability of 1 in 10^{130} is mathematically absurd. No rational people would deduce such, given the facts and there are only 2 options. Therefore the rational person must conclude that the opposite of random events, sequenced events, is more possible, probable and plausible. Sequenced events and organized information decries an intelligent living being which produced life and everything around us.

And don't be fooled by evolutionists. Evolution does not negate the existence of God in any way. In fact, for evolution to be true, you need a creator. You need a living being to produce another living thing. Life doesn't come from inanimate objects. If you think it does, then wait for a grain of sand to turn into a single-celled organism. It will be an exercise in futility. Evolution is the description of the process by which living things develop, it does not address the inception of living things.

The Miller-Urey experiment was performed in 1953 in an effort to prove that life can originate from inanimate matter by chance. Of course, it is mathematically impossible for proteins to appear by chance, so Stanley Miller and Harold Urey attempted to produce the building block of proteins, amino acids. Though it is still used by some up to today as an example of amino acids forming by chance, the experiment was unsuccessful. First, Miller used an incorrect mixture of gases to reproduce the earth's early atmosphere according to *Science* magazine in 1995. Miller also used a mechanism called a cold trap to capture the amino acids that formed in his experiment. He had to capture the amino acids because they would have been destroyed by the electrical spark that he used as an energy source if he didn't capture them. He did not include oxygen, which would have also destroyed the amino acids. And his experiment produced a high level of right-handed amino acids (Life comes from the precise arrangement of only left-handed amino acids. Right-handed amino acids in a protein would render it useless.) But the glaring problem, in my view, is suggesting that something came about my chance, yet you are an intelligent being setting the stage for life to originate. The mere attempt of this experiment is self-contradictory. Those who use this experiment to validate their idea of abiogenesis, the supposed development of living organisms from nonliving matter, are actually proving Intelligent Design. The reason for this experiments failure is because Stanley Miller and Harold Urey were not informed and intelligent enough to create life. And there are other examples of overzealous scientists trying to prove that evolution is true. Their greatest hurdles are the lack of fossil records to validate their claims and the time that it would take for evolution to occur through mutation.

Charles Darwin, the father of the theory of evolution, said "If my theory be true, numberless intermediate varieties, linking most closely all of the species of the same group together must assuredly have existed…Consequently evidence of their former existence could be found only amongst fossil remains." There has been an estimate of 100 million fossils found a century after Darwin's theory and the fossil records which Darwin thought would vindicate him are actually indicting him. Since there is an estimated 3 to 30 million species of animals on earth today and as many as 1 trillion species which are extinct, fossils of these "intermediate varieties" or transitions should be in abundance, but they are not. All the fossils are fully formed.

"The point emerges that if we examine the fossil record in detail, whether at the level of orders or of Species, we find-over and over again-not gradual evolution, but the sudden explosion of one group at the expense of another."

-Evolutionist paleontologist, Derek V. Ager

"A major problem in proving the theory has been the fossil records... This record has never revealed traces of Darwin's hypothetical intermediate variants-instead species appear and disappear abruptly, and this anomaly has fueled the creationist argument that each species was created by God"

-Evolutionist paleontologist, Mark Czarnecki

The Cambrian explosion is an excellent example of animals appearing abruptly without gradual transitions. This explosion occurred 550 million years ago and it has been called the "Biological Big Bang" because it gave rise to most of the animal phyla living today as well as many which are extinct. The record shows that there were jellyfish, sponges and worms before the Cambrian explosion and then BOOM, we see arthropods, modern representatives of insect, crabs, etc; echinoderms, which include modern starfish and sea urchins; chordates, which include vertebrates and so forth. This contradicts Darwin's tree of life, because they appeared fully developed and all of a sudden. In fact, Darwin said, "If numerous species, belonging to the same genera or families, have really started into life all at once, the fact would be fatal to the theory of descent with slow modifications through natural selection."

Though evolutionists greatly downplay the need for fossils, they secretly know that transitional fossils are greatly needed as proof of their claims. There have been frauds and forgeries purposely constructed to fool the public into believing that the case of evolution has been solved. Why would a scientist make forgeries? Why are other scientists so eager and so gullible to accept it hook, line and sinker?

1. The Human Evolution chart- Henry Gee, the chief science writer for "Nature" wrote that "the interval of time that separate fossils are so huge that we cannot say anything definite about their possible connection through ancestry or descent. He also said that "the fossil evidence for human evolution between 10 and 5 million years ago-several thousand generations of living creatures- can be fitted into a small box. He concluded that the conventional pictures of human evolution are a "completely human invention created after the fact, shaped to accord with human prejudices." He added, "to take a line of fossils and claim that they represent a lineage is not scientific hypothesis that can be tested, but an assertion that carries the same validity as a bedtime

story-amusing, perhaps even instructive, but not scientific."

2. Archaeopteryx- the supposed missing link that I like to call the flying snake. Evolutionists said this was evidence that reptiles turned into birds because they believe that birds are descendants of reptiles. Well Larry Martin, a paleontologist, cleared this up in 1985. He said that the archaeopteryx is not the ancestor of the modern bird, or a reptile/bird but a member of a totally extinct group of birds. I call this fraud because this half bird/half reptile story had been taught to school children up to very recently.

3. Archaeoraptor-a complete forgery used to show that birds evolved from dinosaurs/ reptiles. It has the tail of a dinosaur and the forelimbs of a bird. A Chinese paleontologist proved that someone had GLUED a dinosaur tail to a primitive bird. (Apparently its big money in making fake fossils. I wonder, why? A reporter for "Discover" said, "Archaeoraptor was just the tip of the iceberg. There are scores of fake fossils out there.")

4. Bambiraptor-a chicken-sized dinosaur with bird-like characteristics. Paleon-

tologists called it the missing link. It was found to be a turkey.

5. Java man- the part ape/ part man. Well the femur and the skullcap didn't belong to one another. He was actually a human, but as recent as 1994 Time magazine listed Java man as a legitimate evolutionary ancestor of humans.

6. Piltdown man- another forgery of an orangutan jaw attached to a human skull.

7. Nebraska man- another ape/man but this was derived from ONE TOOTH. They drew pictures of the Nebraska ape/man and his ape/man family before they realized that they had the tooth of an extinct PIG.

8. Ida- supposed to be an ancestor of man that turned out to be the fossil of a lemur

9. Lucy- Australopithecus Afarensis is the remains of a primeval ape and not the ancestor of man

10. Ardi- Ardipithecus (ARDI) –like Lucy, Ardi is also the remains of an extinct ape. Both Ardi and Lucy are australopithecines. Australopithecines are a group of extinct apes closely related to modern chimpanzees and orangutans. The Human evolution chart is a mixture of extinct apes and of early

humans, however they all lived together. How can one be the ancestor or the descent of the other when they were contemporaneous?

We begin to see why it's important to have more than hundreds of pieces to a 6 million year old puzzle? The amount of fossils of human ancestry is miniscule in number and they are often skull fragments or teeth. National Geographic hired 4 artists to reconstruct a female figure from 7 bones found in Kenya and they all came out different. One looked like a modern African-American woman, one looked like a werewolf, another had a heavy, gorilla-like brow and the last had a missing forehead and jaws that looked like a beaked dinosaur. The lack of fossil evidence makes it almost impossible to reconstruct these figures. One anthropologists said that it's like trying to reconstruct the plot of "War and Peace" using thirteen random pages from the book.

My point in itemizing these things is not to show that evolution is false, but to show that some people who subscribe to the beliefs of evolution deem it necessary to doctor evidence to support their beliefs because they would like to eliminate God from the picture. I also would like to show that evolution needs God to fill its gaps. Its supporters have been unable to provide fossil records of transitional animals, sea animals beginning to grow lungs or arms or legs. They only provide examples of fully formed animals and place them in the middle of a chart of two or more fully formed animals and say that this is the evidence for transition. This is their interpretation, not legitimate proof. 99% of all species are extinct. These fully formed animals are more than likely a member of an extinct species and not an example of transition. Without true intermediate variations, it is little wonder why some remain skeptical. Though some atheists use evolution to discredit or discount God, it is apparent that they have huge gaps in their beliefs. They continue to find completely developed animals which points towards a creator.

What is confusing is that some would think that the opposite of fully developed animals, animals evolving over time would exclude God. Both fully developed and evolving to fully development animals require a creator. And because evolution is a process it necessitates a cause. It is a mechanical system in need of a personal cause. The Theory of Evolution's gap is personified in the fossil records, but it is also personified in its greatest component, mutation.

Mutations are a rearranging or deletion of the code in DNA. Evolutionists say that through millions of years and numerous mutations in our DNA, all species of animals on earth have evolved. As I have shown, fossil records show fully formed animals. Of the one trillion species that have been on earth, there are no examples of the mutating of one species into another or a species growing an organ foreign to its DNA. DNA replicates itself with 99.9999999% accurate. It has a proofreading system which checks and double checks it's work. DNA also repairs itself and sexual reproduction does not continue the mutation, it corrects it. In addition to this, most mutations are deleterious or of no effect. They are random. And positive mutations are extremely rare and generally not positive to the individual. They do not emerge as a result of necessity or as a result of stimulus. And most importantly, mutation does not cause new information in the DNA. It only corrupts the information already there. Therefore you will never find a man with a bee-stringer or wings, because there is no information for the formation of these things in his DNA.

The only observed mutations in real life or in fossils are of organs already in the DNA which arise like a sixth finger or a third nostril or something like that. If it is true that mutation causes new information then I want to see a human with some animal features. There are 6.8 billion people on earth and 100 billion who have lived. Why can't we find these things? There have been 1 trillion species of animals, which means a googol amount of animals on earth. Where is the evidence of DNA forming new organs, not already in their DNA? And even if this is true, the probability that the right mutations occurred at the right time is astronomical. Again mutations are completely random and they cannot be induced by circumstance. This positive mutation must slip through every obstacle of replication, reading, proofreading, and reproduction. And to compound matters, it is in need of a multitude of other positive mutations that can pass these obstacles and exist simultaneously with it.

Consider the fish-like creature from which evolutionists say all terrestrial life emerged. This creature needed lungs to live on land, but it also needs feet to walk. And it needed every facet of the anatomy for those parts to function all at once, because anyone of these would have been a hindrance, not a help to the animal, thus causing the animal to die and most certainly discontinue the passing down of a negative mutation from generation to generation. Therefore one mutation is not enough. You need a larynx, a trachea, bronchial tubes, nerves, brain signals, etc. Not to mention, all that is required to walk. This idea of evolution requires a MULTITUDE of POSITIVE mutations occurring simultaneously, and all these "miracle" mutations must pass to generation after generation. These multitudinous positive mutations must work together and not be harmful to the subjects.

"In a paper titled "The Inadequacy of Neo-Darwinian Evolution As a Scientific Theory," Professor Murray Eden from the MIT (Massachusetts Institute of Technology) Faculty of Electrical Engineering showed that if it required a mere six mutations to bring about an adaptive change, this would occur by chance only once in a billion years - while, if two dozen genes were involved, it would require 10,000,000,000 years, which is much longer than the age of the Earth. Even if we assume that mutations were effective and beneficial in complex organs and structures requiring more than one mutation to occur at the same time, mathematicians still say the problem of time is an acute dilemma for Darwinists. Even Professor of Paleontology George G. Simpson, one of the most unrepentant Darwinists, clearly states that it would take an infinite length of time for five mutations to happen at the same time. An infinite amount of time means zero probability.

The evolutionist George G. Simpson has performed another calculation regarding the mutation claim in question. He admitted that in a community of 100 million individuals we assume to produce a new generation every day, a positive outcome from mutations would only take place once every 274 billion years. That number is many times greater the age of the Earth, estimated at 4.5 billion years. These, of course, are all calculations assuming that mutations have a positive effect of that new generations gave rise to. But no such assumption applies in the real world."(Harun Yahya, "The Idea that 'Mutations cause Evolution' is a Falsehood")

So far we have come to the conclusion that for any system or process to begin, a cause is required. And for evolution to be true, it is in dire need of an intervener. Therefore this is not a God of the Gaps argument. We are not simply inserting God in the gaps of nature and the universe's existence based on ignorance. This conclusion is based upon evidence. This evidence necessitates God's existence. We have also found that anything that begins to exist has a cause and that life comes from life. It is clear that a First Cause is necessary for our existence in this universe. No thinking person can refute this fact. And finally we have found that life does not come from random events, but sequenced purposeful creation from an intelligent being. Atheism and agnosticism are untenable for any rational person. Deism is their only logical alternative.

The End of Deism

"There is a wide agreement which on the physical side of the sciences approaches unanimity that the stream of knowledge is headed towards a NON-MECHANICAL reality that the universe begins to look more like a great thought than a great machine. Mind no longer appears to be an accidental intruder in the realm of matter. We are beginning to suspect that we ought to hail Mind as the creator and the governor of the realm of matter. Not our individual mind, but the Mind out of which atoms and the entire universe has grown to exist as thoughts." -Sir James Hopwood Jeans (an English physicist, astronomer and mathematician)

Deism is the belief in the existence of a supreme being, specifically of a creator who does not intervene in the universe. This being created the universe and abandons it. Deists typically deny the existence of miracles and of revelation; however these ideas should be abandoned with more reflection on God and his creation. Miracles and revelations are closely related, but first let us tackle the idea of miracles. Miracles are supernatural events. In order for a person to become a deist, he must already believe in miracles. The existence of this creator is beyond the realm of nature, i.e. it is a miracle. The creation of the universe is a miracle. It is not natural for nothing to turn into something. It is not natural for an explosion to construct the ever-expanding universe. It is not natural for things to develop and evolve over time. Some scientists suggest that life emerged on earth 3.5 billion years ago, 1 billion years after the formation of earth. 3.5 billion years and one second ago life did not exist. Therefore a miracle occurred at that time. When we realize that life comes from life, we understand that the origin of life must be from God. Therefore, 1 billion years after the formation of the earth and 9 billion years after the formation of the universe the Creator created life. Does the deist believe that God intervened in the course of the universe? No, the deist understands that these phenomenon are the plans of God and they merely came to fruition at a given time period in history. But they are miracles, nonetheless. So what about revelation?

Another miracle, the Cambrian explosion occurred 550 million years ago and it gave rise to most of the animal phyla living today. The deist must assume that this was in the plans of intelligent God or that

God accidently knocked over the ingredients to create the universe 14 billion years ago and life miraculously formed by random chance (a notion which we have already dismissed as ridiculous). The point that I am making is that deism need not be in disagreement with the theist on the issue of revelation. That man has discovered the evidence of the Big Bang, and the Biological Big Bang is evidence of revelation. God has made these things discoverable for man, to reveal to man that he is real.

For instance, think about the information in DNA. Information is only useful to those who understand it. God made this code for us to read and see his signature. HE MADE THE INFORMATION IN DNA DISCOVERABLE TO MAN, THE MOST INTELLIGENT LIFE FORM ON EARTH. Evolutionist atheists suggest that we are merely byproducts of the Big Bang and that we are insignificant in the midst of our great galaxy. The fact that the Creator made a point to communicate to us contradicts their assumption and it contradicts the assumption of the deist that God does not communicate to us. It is apparent that belief in miracles and revelations are unavoidable with a belief in the creator.

The revelations found in creation are indirect revelations, but what about direct revelations sent to man? Deists acknowledge the existence of morality and the difference between right and wrong deeds. They assert that God wants man to live righteously, but how do they come to this conclusion and how does a deist determine what God deems is right and wrong? And why does God want man to live righteously? Any answer that a deist gives can only be speculative. He relies on human wisdom to determine right from wrong and to determine why we must live this way.

God has given man reasoning, comprehension and the need for understanding his existence and the existence of everything around him. Just as God has provided for the needs of every plant and animal on earth, God provides for man's need of understanding. God also provides for man's need for justice, which includes punishment and rewards. And he provides these things in a manner that does not require speculation. God's decrees are unequivocal.

Some deists will acknowledge that God has given man a conscience which steers him in the direction of morality, but so too has God given man instinct and at some point these two conflict. Man has a natural desire for selfishness. He wants blessings to be shed upon himself and those whom he cares for. Selflessness and self-restraint are totally against man's instinct, but in agreement with his conscience. But one's conscience is but a compass to righteousness, it is not enough. Consider the rules that we live by in everyday life. If our conscience was enough there would be no need for laws, amendments, and constitutions to be written. These decrees are written as concrete rules that one must live by. One cannot go to court and suggest that he did not know that it was wrong to steal or to kill. He cannot appeal to his own sense of right and wrong because there are official rules established that he must live by. The same is true for God's revelation. The creator of man is best to determine what is right and wrong for him, how he is to conduct himself and how he should relate to his Creator. Because God reveals his will through revelations, man cannot hide under the guise of ignorance of the laws and he cannot use his own wisdom to determine what God wants. Can not the Creator of the universe express himself to his creation? As Sheikh Abdur Raheem suggests

"You say that you want to pay respect to your mother and father and you take them to a rock concert. You aren't respecting them. You are following your own desires. In like manner, you can't decide how you want to honor God. He tells you how to honor him. You do not decide what is good, God does. You don't go to your boss and tell him what work you are going to do. He tells you your job."

As the organized information in DNA displays the signature of God, so too should his direct revelation to man. This revelation should be vigorously scrutinized to verify that it is indeed from God. It should be a testament to its author. It should reflect his nature of mercy, forgiveness, love, and justice. It should be a revelation replete with truth in diverse stratospheres of knowledge, but it should be devoid of contradictions. And most importantly, it should be a guidance to righteousness and a deterrent from wickedness. (No book fulfills these criteria better than the Holy Qur'an. The content of the Qur'an itself is proof of God. For scientific evidence in the Qur'an of God, see my book, "Islam is the Truth"). God's revelation should touch your heart, your mind and your soul. Your soul is the real you. Let us explore our true selves.

"The quantum theory finds that the smallest units of matter are not physical objects, they are actually ideas." -Werner Heisenberg (a German theoretical physicist who was awarded the 1932 Nobel Prize in Physics for the creation of quantum mechanics.)

The universe and everything and everyone in it are made up of mostly NOTHING. Remember that we have found that the universe came from nothing. Well it is still made of mostly empty space. Approximately 74% of the universe is "nothing" or dark energy. 22% is dark matter or particles that we cannot see and only 4% of the universe is baryonic matter or the things that we can see, touch, hear or smell. And even those things are mostly NOTHING. Atoms consist mainly of empty space.

The volume of an atom is made up of a tiny nucleus, the electron orbiting it and the empty space between them. The electrons are traveling at a tremendous distance and speed. The matter's solidity is an illusion caused by the electric fields created by this orbit. Compound this illusion with the fact that everything that we see, taste, touch, smell and hear is nothing but an electrical signal in our brain and the world around us has to be redefined.

Did you know that we experience everything every day as an electrical signal in our brain? When you touch this book, your fingers are sending a signal to the brain, your brain interprets that signal and you perceive a book. The same is true for your sight. The words that you read travel from your eye as an electric signal that your brain interprets as you read. You do not actually taste with your tongue, you do not smell with your nose nor do you hear with your ears. All these body parts are simply tools used to send electric signals to your brain to be interpreted. This is a scientific fact. One can easily verify this fact when they ponder their dreams. In your dreams, you can eat a delicious meal, listen to an orchestra, watch a movie and even die in your dreams and you have the same feelings that you have when you are awake. In your dreams, you can hear an orchestra without using your ears, or see a movie with your eyes closed, how is that so? It is your brain interpreting electric signals, but your brain is also a tool. The brain interprets that signal, but it is also a product of this material world and it perceives nothing. What actually perceives this world and everything around us is our soul. Your body is simply the vehicle used to travel and experience this world. Our soul is our true selves. Our immaterial dreams, our immaterial thoughts, our immaterial feelings, like love, compassion, and anger are from our immaterial soul.

Did you know that every 7 years every atom of your body is replaced with other atoms? If every part of our body is a replacement then how are we the same people? If you change every part, nut and bolt of your car, is it the same car? No, it is a different car, rebuilt to look like the original. The reason that we are the same after 7 years is because our souls have not been replaced. Our soul is our true selves. And our souls, as immaterial entities, are another proof of the immaterial Creator. This soul is directly from God into man to produce life. This is why you can put together every part of a human being, like Dr. Frankenstein, but you will not be able to give this body life. This life is a gift of God. When we put all of these things into perspective, it is apparent that we are put on this earth for a reason and a purpose. God has set a stage, this planet, and he has given us a vehicle, our body, to travel and experience this life, but why? Our purpose is to be just rulers of this world. We are to be righteous beings, in our dealings with each other and in our management of nature and everything in our grasp. Being righteous is a great form of worship to God. And God implants in our soul an inclination towards righteousness. God starts man off with a clean slate, a clear path and a conscience, as a compass, to guide him towards what is right and God, throughout history, sends exemplary figures to demonstrate the proper path towards his service. And who can better address man's problems than God, the maker of man and of man's circumstances?

"In brief, we DON'T BELONG TO THE MATERIAL WORLD THAT SCIENCE HAS CONSTRUCTED FOR US. We, the awareness of being ourselves, are not part of it. We are outside, we are only spectators. The reason why we believe that we are in it, that we belong to this picture, is that are bodies are in the picture. And that is the only way of our minds communicating with it." -Erwin Schrödinger (an Austrian physicist and theoretical biologist who received the Nobel Prize in Physics in 1933.)

At this point, I think that mere deism is insufficient in providing the answers that man seeks, as well as a definitive direction that man must move in. If we ponder deeply enough, we will find that we all believe in the miracles of God, in revelations from God, in the unseen and in the need for the guidance from God to keep our souls, our conscience and our deeds in unison. These things put to rest the question of a personal God. The existence of our soul, alone, is ample proof that the Creator has great interest in his creation. In fact, God has invested a bit of himself in man and he allows man the opportunity to multiply or squander this investment with his deeds on earth.

Now we have discussed the evidence of the spirit of God in man and that our soul is the means in which we understand and interact with the world around us. I have also explained that our thoughts and dreams are proof of our soul. But my explanation can be taken a bit further. If we think about it, how many of our dreams are good dreams? In dreams, most people feel anxiety. More negative feelings are induced in our dreams than positive feelings. And even the positive feelings are often a result of something we have done in our dreams which is morally wrong. Most dreams are senseless and bizarre and they are filled with regrettable deeds, done by you or someone else. They are like deleted scenes in a movie. You could have done these things and you can do them in real life. People wake up in a cold sweat or they are relieved that this was only a dream. This is man's opportunity to see and experience the results of his actions without the consequences. The soul in man is what is actually viewing his dreams and learning from them. This is but a gift from God to help man avoid the pitfalls of life.

Another unexplained phenomenon of man is déjà vu or the feeling that you have experienced a certain event before. But this definition insinuates that a person is experiencing something in the present which they have already experienced in the past. I do not think this is what people mean when they say they have experienced déjà vu. I think what they mean to say is that they have foreknowledge of the event that is happening in the present that they only become aware of when it actually happened. In other words, they knew the future. If you experience déjà vu while you are with two of your friends, you must realize that you knew in your subconscious beforehand that they were going to be the age, the height and the weight that they were before the experience. You knew what haircut they would have and what clothes that they would wear. But the problem is that your mind can only perceive what you have experienced and what you are experiencing right now. You may guess that a certain situation will occur, but how did you subconsciously know something that happened in the future? (This is not to be confused or used to try and predict the future. Déjà vu is not under our control) God gives you a glimpse of the future through your spirit. Déjà vu is another proof of the soul of man given to him by God, who views the past, present and future, not in sequence, but as one. The only question that remains is why must we insist that God is one?

The end of polytheism

The idea of polytheism giving birth to monotheism is one which has been purported as a fact of history. It was conceived by Sir Edward Burnett Tylor. He surmised that man first was an animist (one who believes that spirits exist in everything including humans, rocks, plants and thunder), then a polytheist and finally a monotheist. Those, like Tylor, who believe in evolution, see this process as an example of the gradual improvement and advancement of human thinking. (I am certain that many of them believe that the inevitable next step from the belief in one God is the belief in no god at all.) However, this idea has come under great scrutiny.

Authors like John Mbiti in his book, "General Manifestations of African Religiosity" and Arthur C. Custance in his book, "Evolution of Creation?"

raise several points which question the common belief that monotheism is an evolution from polytheism. Mbiti points out that the people of Africa have, from their inception (also humanity's inception), been a monotheistic people and they have been given the misnomer of heathens and pagans by those who mistook the rituals to their ancestors as worship. Mr. Custance went so far as to point out the monotheism of the ancient Sumerians, the ancient Egyptians, as well as the ancient Chinese. Friedrich Max Muller, a famous German scholar suggested that Greek, Roman and Indian mythology did not originate as polytheism. Muller in "Lectures on the Science of Language" said

"Mythology, which was the bane of the ancient world, is in truth a disease of language. A myth means a word, but a word which, from being a name or an attribute, has been allowed to assume a more substantial existence. Most of the Greek, the Roman, the Indian, and other heathen gods are nothing but poetical names, which were gradually allowed to assume divine personality never contemplated by their original inventors. ... Eos was the name of dawn before she became a goddess, the wife of Tithonos, or the dying day. Fatum, or Fate, meant originally what had been spoken; and before Fate became a power, even greater than Jupiter, it meant that which had once been spoken by Jupiter, and could never be changed - not even by Jupiter himself.... Zeus originally meant the bright heaven, in Sanskrit Dyaus; and many of the stories told of him as the supreme god, had a meaning only as told originally of the bright heaven, the Danae of old, kept by her father in the dark prison of winter…"

Muller also wrote in his book, "A History of Ancient Sanskrit Literature" that "There is a monotheism that precedes the polytheism of the Veda; and even in the invocation of the innumerable gods the remembrance of a God, one and infinite, breaks through the mist of idolatrous phraseology like the blue sky that is hidden by passing clouds."

Edward Tylor's favorite pupil, Andrew Lang was once an advocate of Tylor's doctrine, but when he was confronted with evidence to the contrary, Lang became a staunch adversity to Tylor's findings. Lang wrote a book about his revised stance called "The Making of Religion." He used "the startling discoveries of A.W. Howitt (Australian anthropologist and naturist) concerning the Supreme Being of the South-East Australian tribes. He made use…of facts from the Bushmen, Hottentotts, Zulu, Yao, the West African people, the Tierra del Fuegians and somewhat more extensively the North American Indians."

In 1912, Wilhelm Schmidt published his mammoth "Ursprung Der Gottesidee" (The Origin of the Concept of God). Still more data kept pouring in, so he published another volume, and another and another until, 1955, he had accumulated more than 4,000 pages of evidence in a total of 12 large volumes! The entire 13th chapter of Schmidt's

(book) is devoted to quotations from dozens of anthropologists, showing that acceptance of Schmidt's research was virtually universal."
-"Eternity in Their Hearts: Startling Evidence of Belief in the One True God in Hundreds of Cultures Throughout the World," Don Richardson

Don Richardson, in his aforementioned book, enumerates his research of ancient monotheism. He lists "ten peoples totaling more than 3 million men and women"

1. The Incans who called God, Viracocha-The Lord, The Omnipotent Creator of all things
2. The Santal called God, Thakur Jiu-The Genuine God
3. The Kachin called God, Karai Kasang- A benign Supernatural Being "whose shape or form exceeds man's ability to comprehend—also called Hpan Wa Ningsang- The Glorious One who creates or Che Wa Ningchang-The One who knows
4. The Lahu called God, Gui'sha- Creator of all things
5. The Wa called God,Wiyeh-The True God
6. The Kui people of Thailand and Burma believed in one God.
7. The Lisu of China were monotheists.
8. The Naga people called God, Chepo-Thuru or Gwang-The God who sustains everything
9. The Mizo called God, Pathian-The One Supreme God or Holy Father
10.The Karen called God, Y'wa-The True God (whose name predates Judaism). They also had

hymns about this True God. For example:

Y'wa is eternal, his life is long!
One aeon-he does not die!
Two aeons-he does not die!
He is perfect in meritorious attributes!
Aeons follow eons-he dies not!

and

Who created the world in the beginning?
Y'wa created the world in the beginning!
Y'wa appointed everything!
Y'wa is unsearchable!

Richardson asserts that even Zeus was the general name used for the one Supreme God until the Greeks gave Him parents. He also shows that the Canaanites, long before the arrival of Judaism, were monotheistic calling God, El Elyon or God the Most High.

Now we must bear in mind that 105 billion people have lived on this earth and only 2% of them lived before the Prophet Jesus (pbuh) was born. Therefore the over 3 million people Richardson has documented as having a monotheistic foundation combined with the findings of Schmidt, Lang, Muller, Constance, and Mbiti should put this issue to rest. It becomes clear that "primitive" man was not so primitive in his initial understanding of God.

(It is the Qur'an which insists that man has been living righteous under one God since his inception and man has deviated from this path.) Perhaps his desire to move himself closer to God or God closer to him lead him to add gods in between he and the supreme God. One need to look no further than the doctrine of the Christian Trinity to identify the possibility that polytheism can devolved from monotheism. The Trinity, which stresses that God is personified in three persons, the Father, the Son and the Holy Spirit, was formulated, and solidified over 300 years after the Prophet Jesus (pbuh) declared that God is one (Mark 12:29) and that no one has seen his form, nor heard his voice at ANY TIME (John 5:37) [My book entitled "There is no Trinity" fully illustrates that the Christian Trinity is a deviation from the monotheism of Abraham, Moses, etc (pbut)]. However the question of which came first, the chicken or the egg, does little to answer why God is one. So we must address this issue.

In Surah 67:3-4 of the Qur'an, man is asked to consider the harmonious governing of the universe. The Qur'an draws our attention to the fact that the reason that we can identify laws of the universe so precisely is because the universe has one governor. If there were more than one God, then each god would have to depend on another god to make the system work. Just like the conflicts of mythology, one god would lord over another because one is in need of the other god's power. Man must understand that the laws of the universe and the laws of nature are constant because there is but one Creator and sustainer.

Also multiplicity is only possible in the finite world. In the infinite realm there cannot be two infinites. This is a contradiction in terms. In order for there to be two, one would have to be distinct from the other in some way. Two or more of something implies space which is restricted by one's own perimeters and by the amount of space taken up by the other infinite being, in which case it is not infinite.

The Qur'an insists that man should not go to extremes in his religion and only say of God what is true. Similar to Occam's razor ("entities must not be multiplied beyond necessity"), the Qur'an suggests that one hold on to what must be true and eliminate conjecture. It is required that there be at least one God, and belief in any more gods would be superfluous. The Qur'an also postulates that man is bound by a singular moral authority. The Prophet Joseph (pbuh) once asked if it is more preferably to worship an assortment of gods or the one true God, which encompasses the abilities of all the other gods (12:39). This is like asking, do you prefer one president or ten? The rational person would choose one. Just as the presence of multiple gods would lead to disharmony in the governing of the universe, so too would it lead to a conflicting view of morality and obedience.

The Right God

So what can we deduce about the nature of God? We can deduce that he is a God of morality. If he provides morals, he must also provide justice because justice is a requisite for morality. Therefore we can be certain, that all of our deeds and misdeeds will be calling into account. He gives man free will, which demonstrates that he is a God that gives countless opportunities for man's redemption. He is tolerant, because he allows for mistakes without immediate ramifications. This suggests forgiveness and mercy. He is loving and compassionate. He gives man more than what he needs, which suggests an affinity. He also grants man privilege to give and receive love, and compassion. God does good for the sake of good only and he wants man to do the same. This God receives no benefit if man is benevolent or malevolent, thus the giving of his bounty is solely for goodness sake. He is ageless. No beginning and no ending. He is self sustaining. But is He all powerful? Not in the sense that He can do all things, but He has power over all of his creation. Because of the Trinity, many Christians are forced to postulate that God can do anything, since in their minds, He can make three equal one and He can be mortal and immortal simultaneously. This is not the case. If God can do anything, then he can do foolish things. If he can do anything then he can die, which contradicts his immortality. Can he sin? According to the Bible, he cannot lie (Titus 1:2) and he cannot be tempted in any sin (James 1:13). In other words, He is UNABLE to sin, thus He cannot do all things. God has a nature that cannot be broken. His nature is of good and godly things. He does not lower himself to sin or to become the equivalent of his creation. There is no circumstance which would require God to become his own creation. God is able to solve the problems of his creation as God, not a cow, or an elephant or as a man.

In Islam, only God is God and when God declares a matter he just wills it into being. He doesn't have to become a human being. Becoming a part of his creation is degrading and downgrading himself. As a self-sustaining God, he is never vulnerable at any times. He doesn't need sleep and he doesn't need food. In order for God to BECOME a mortal human being, he must no longer be an immortal God. The word "become" denotes a transformation. It is as if the sun became a period in this book. If it did, would planets still orbit it? Will it still support life on earth? No, because it is a period now. Therefore, if God BECAME a man, he is no longer all-knowing, he is no longer self-sustaining, etc. We must keep in mind that God is the apex for all that is good because the magnitude of his magnanimous reach cannot be approached by the collective of his creation, let alone one of his creatures. Man's highest position can never be described as godlike, but perhaps godly. The exaltation of his creation to a godlike level is essentially the denigration of the Creator.

In Conclusion

Everyone believes in something. Belief guides our every action. We believe that when we turn a door knob, we can open a door, so we do it. We believe when we turn the key in the ignition, the car will turn on, so we do it. The more evidence to believe a thing, the more confidently we perform an action. In like manner, the more that we are convinced of God's existence, the more we will act upon that knowledge. If we are convinced that God is real and he will hold us accountable for our deeds and misdeeds, the more righteous we will become. If you knew for certain that your employer could see your every move, wouldn't you perform at your best? This is why it is imperative to understand that God is real and he does see our every move. Belief in God has a correlation with our health because it is natural for man to believe in God. In this booklet,

I use facts of science to prove the existence of God. This is because in most instances the facts are not in question, but the interpretation of the facts is what is in question. My position is that science is providing the evidence for God.

My position on atheism and agnosticism have very little to do with the actions of those who accept these beliefs and more to do with their actual beliefs. The belief that life and man are accidents, that his every thought and action are essentially inconsequential, that there is no purpose to life, that man seeks justice but there is no true justice, that morality is subjective, that love and relationships are nothing more than byproducts of evolution; these beliefs are dismal in my view. Famous atheist and neuroscientist, Sam Harris has written a book on morality, but a moral atheist is an oxymoron. It is as meaningless as a moral mosquito. Atheists believe that humans aren't anything special as theists do. They think that our existence is accidental or coincidental, therefore our every action is essentially inconsequential, even our morals. They are a byproduct of an unintelligible event. And since morality is subjective, justice is also subjective meaning that in some cases or in some societies or at some time murder is acceptable behavior, that stealing is acceptable behavior, etc. Richard Dawkins recently said that there is no logical connection between atheism and heinous crimes. I beg to differ. Specifically because atheism sees man as an animal making morals and justice subjective, it gives license for any behavior to be considered instinct. Animals have instinct. Dawkins described man as an evolved African Ape, as such his every action is in effect his animal instincts at work. How exactly do we litigate instincts? Or more importantly, why should we litigate instincts? It would be like holding ants responsible for "stealing" your picnic food, or a snake for "murdering" a rat or a bee for "robbing" a flower of its pollen. These animals are acting out of instinct, thus their actions aren't punishable. From an atheist's standpoint, the same should be true of an evolved "African ape." Of course, they can never concede this point. They will always be in pursuit of righteousness because there is something in them which demands morality, justice, purpose and understanding.

Self-sacrifice, selflessness, self-restraint, sympathy, empathy, love, mercy and forgiveness are human traits far removed from animals and their instincts. Animals generally let their weak die, or kill them themselves. Thus natural selection happens because they allow it to. In fact, morality and justice are hindrances to natural selection and evolution in nature. Humans protect the weak. They make laws and rules to insure their safety. They feel compassion for the needy. Theists believe this sense of morality is given to man purposely, by his Creator, because man is to be the viceroy of this planet. Man is given the capacity to destroy this planet or to rejuvenate it. No other being has this ability and if they did, none of them could use that ability ON PURPOSE and for that purpose. The atheist's belief falls on the side of coincidence. They think that it is a coincidence that we have morals and a conscience, and the ability to destroy or rejuvenate the planet and that these morals are solely for our survival. I think that they are for man to do good for the sake of good. They are for man to be a caretaker over this planet, because he is given the ability and the knowledge to do it. It is because we have a purpose and because morals are not subjective and because justice is not just something that we seek, but something that we all will find, that I am certain that there is a Creator who has deliberately empowered us.

Man is also endowed with consciousness. Not only consciousness, but man has distinctive consciousness. If man is created from the same substances by pure chance, with no intelligent intervention, how could people possibly have different personalities? A human can make robots with different functions, but how likely is it that robots accidentally form by themselves from the same materials and they all have different functions? The atheist calls this a coincidence, by this he actually means a miracle took place. And they, like the deists, most certainly believe in miracles. The formation of this universe from nothing is the description of a miracle. That one does not believe in God, only means that they believe in a magic trick (the formation of the universe) without a magician. His belief in life coming from inanimate objects is also a miracle. The atheists answer to everything is random chance and time. He places his faith in these two things and with them all things are possible. Yet he ignores the possibility of God. I wonder how many coincidences it takes for someone to realize that these occurrences are not coincidences at all. If you stand under a tree and an apple hits you, that is an incident. If you stand under the tree and an apple hits you again, that is a coincidence. If this happens a third time, someone is throwing apples at you.

The universe was created from nothing (this alone is more than sufficient for most rational people), an explosion constructed the universe, the planets and sun aligned so perfectly and precisely to allow for the sustaining of life on earth, the precision of the gravitational pull on earth, the precise level of gases in our atmosphere, the earth's tilt, its orbit and rotation around the sun and its distance from the moon are all conducive to life. All these things are coincidences, lucky chances to one who rejects God. There once was no life and then abruptly life appeared on earth. Another coincidence! More organized information than what is to be found in an entire collection of encyclopedias are accumulated in microscopic DNA, which is smaller than the tip of a needle. This is a coincidence! Proteins appeared, despite the 1 in 10 with 125 zeros odds for a single protein to be produces randomly. Coincidence! The Cambrian Explosion, the lack of fossils for proof of evolution, the emergence of multiple mutations simultaneously are all coincidences!! Consciousness, human conscience, morality, justice, love and sovereignty are all mere coincidences!!! Who really is the gullible faith based follower?

In spite of several attempts at a rebuttal, William Paley's watchmaker analogy still stands. If you find a watch in the desert, its existence requires a watchmaker. The alternative is that a lump of gold rested in a position which allowed for it to melt, be molded and shaped into a size that can fit on your wrist. Simultaneously, the plastic top of the watch is being shaped and molded. No one knows how this happened without an intelligent being to do this because plastic does not exist in the natural state. It is synthesized from petroleum. While this is happening (by magic), the inside components of a watch are also forming into shape. The small and large arms of the watch construct randomly from nature, the numbers 1 through 12 appear from nature, and the hash marks between the numbers take shape, luckily they share the exact same size. Finally we have a whisk of wind, or a tornado which combines all these components in perfect order. This series of coincidences compose a working mechanism that contains organized information (the sequence of numbers) and tells time. The fact that these miraculous events are needed to produce a simple watch, should make us give deeper thought to the production of cells, DNA, protein, amino acids, the human body, the human mind, and life itself. The atheist and the agnostic are always on the side of believing the improbable and according to Borel's law the mathematically IMPOSSIBLE. The adherence to their beliefs is outrageously untenable, whereas the existence of God is undeniable. That he exists is not an opinion, but a FACT. He is ALLAH (the God), the One, the Irresistible (Qur'an 39:4)

FIVE PILLARS OF ISLAM

1. Shahadatain- This is the oath that every person must say and believe in order to be a Muslim. It is as follows: I bear witness that there is no god, but ALLAH and I bear witness that Muhammad is his Messenger. This is the most important tenants of Islam. Islam is vehement in its insistence that God is one, without partners or associates and this God (in Arabic ALLAH) communicates his will to mankind through exemplary men in history. These men are Prophets and/or Messengers of God and they include Adam, Abraham, Noah, Jacob, Isaac, Ishmael, Moses, Aaron, Lot, David, Solomon and Jesus (pbut). The last of the Prophets of God is Muhammad (pbuh) and he has been given a message to convey to all of humanity. That message is the same message given by all of God's prophets, submission to the will of God. The Arabic word for submission to God's will is Islam.

2. Worship- called Salat in Arabic; it is the prayer Muslims give to God/ALLAH five times a day. It is not the traditional prayer of requests for God. It is structured for the praise and remembrance of God throughout the day.

3. Charity- called Zakat in Arabic; it is the obligation on every Muslim to give 2.5% of his wealth to the poor, the sick and for travelers in need. God gives people opportunities to help others. One of these opportunities is with one's wealth, but it also includes sharing your time and effort to help others. In fact, a smile or a kind word is an act of charity and worship in Islam.

4. Fasting-During the month of Ramadhan, all Muslims are required to restrict their consumption of food and drink from sunrise to sunset. They also abstain from sexual relations with their spouse from sunrise to sunset. This is a lesson in self-restraint and a way in which one can feel the struggle of those less-fortunate. This is also a time to reacquaint one's self with the Qur'an and to renew their commitment to following the decrees set forth in Islam.

5. Hajj- This is the largest pilgrimage in the world. It is a pilgrimage to the holy city of Mecca and it is required of all able bodied Muslims, who can afford it, at least once in their life. Every Muslim, whether rich or poor, black or white, short or tall are all brothers and sisters. We all pray in unison in one direction, at the same time and using the similar words in praise to God and this pilgrimage is the ultimate manifestation of the oneness of the 1.8 billion Muslim community.

ABOUT THE AUTHOR

Mr. Campbell was raised attending both the Christian Church and the Muslim Mosque. He was always inquisitive about religion. Around the age of 14, he decided that Islam was the path for him. However, he was rather secretive about his belief due to the negative perception many had of the religion. When Islam became the topic of any discussion, he maintained the Islamic sympathizer role as the son of a Muslim, while being careful not to be identified as a Muslim himself. The stigma surrounding Islam and Muslims only intensified throughout the years, but so too did his desire to announce to the world that ISLAM IS THE TRUTH. Throughout his life, he had engage others in discussions on religion and a little over three years ago he realized that the issues that were raised in debate and in dialogue were issues which warranted extensive details, evidence and explanations. Drawing from all the books, lectures, and debates he come in contact with, and all the talks with Muslims, Christians, Jews, Hindus, atheists and agnostics, he set out to write one book which would convince all of the truth about the God of the universe. This one book blossomed into eight books which are written with the primary goal of proving the validity of Islam. It is with his sincerest effort that he wrote these books, with the hope that all readers will set aside their preconceived ideas and have an open mind.

I.D. Campbell

Made in United States
Orlando, FL
01 March 2022